REBEL RHYT
SHANE MACGOWAN SAGA

Beyond the Fairy-tale:Unveiling the Untold Story of a Musical Maverick, The Life, Lyrics, and Legacy of Shane MacGowan

Thomas K. Clinton

Copyright Page

2023 by Thomas k. Clinton

All rights reserved. No part of this publication may be reproduced, distributed, or transmitted in any form or by any means, including photocopying, recording, or other electronic or mechanical methods, without the prior written permission of the publisher, except in the case of brief quotations embodied in critical reviews and certain other noncommercial uses permitted by copyright law. For permission requests, write to the publisher at the address below.

This book is a work of fiction/non-fiction. Names, characters, places, and incidents are either products of the author's imagination or are used fictitiously. Any resemblance to actual persons, living or dead, events, or locales is entirely coincidental.

Dedication

For the Music Makers, Dreamers, and Rebels. This book is devoted to individuals who find refuge, inspiration, and resistance in Shane MacGowan's wild rhythms.

Preface

A tale is hidden in the heart of every tune, and a journey is hidden in the spirit of every artist. "Rebel Rhythms: The Shane MacGowan Saga" is more than just a collection of chords and words; it's an investigation into the unique life that inspired them. This book attempts to unravel the tapestry of Shane MacGowan, a musical maverick whose rebellious spirit crossed genres, broke standards, and left an everlasting impact on the annals of music history.

Expect a trip that goes beyond the surface of chart-topping singles and into the depths of personal challenges, artistic achievements, and the enduring legacy of a punk-folk pioneer as we delve into the pages that follow. "Rebel Rhythms" allows you to travel the melodies that defined a period and find the undiscovered stories that echo inside Shane MacGowan's chords.

Allow the music to play and the pages to flip as we begin on a musical journey through Shane MacGowan's life, lyrics, and legacy.

THOMAS K. CLINTON

TABLE OF CONTENTS

Copyright Page ··· 2

Dedication ··· 3

Preface ·· 4

Introduction ··· 9

    Background and Childhood ····························· 9

    Musical Career Overview ······························· 10

    Importance and Impact ·································· 10

Chapter 1: ··· 14

Rebel Roots ··· 14

    Family History ··· 14

    Early Musical Influences and Inspiration ············ 16

Chapter 2 ·· 19

Pogue Mahone's Period (1982-1984) ····················· 19

    The Pogue Mahone's Formation ······················· 19

    The Pogues' Evolution ··································· 20

    Musical Influences and Style ··························· 21

    "Red Roses for Me" Debut Album ···················· 22

Chapter 3 25

Songwriting Prowess of MacGowan 25

    Theme and Songwriting Process 25

    Classic Songs and Lyrics 27

    Inter-Pogues Collaborations 28

Chapter 4 31

Difficulties and Breaks 31

    Personal Struggles of MacGowan 31

    Effect on Band Dynamics and Interruptions 32

    Medical Concerns and Rehabilitation 33

Chapter 5 35

New York Fairy-tale and Commercial Success 35

    Development of "Fairy-tale of New York" 35

    Publication and Reception 36

    Commercial and Critical Success 38

Chapter 6 41

Collaborations and the Pope's Era (1994-2005) 41

    The Popes' Formation 41

    Projects with Johnny Depp and Sinéad O'Connor · 42

    Musical Style and Evolution 43

Chapter 7 · 47
Afterlife and Legacy · 47
Pogues Reunions and Final Years · · · · · · · · · · · · · · · · 47
Contemporary Music Influence · · · · · · · · · · · · · · · · · 48

Chapter 8 · 52
Recognition, Awards, and Cultural Impact · · · · · · · · · · · · · 52
Awards and Recognition · 52
Cultural Influence and Impact · · · · · · · · · · · · · · · · · 54

Chapter 9 · 58
Reflections and Personal Life · · · · · · · · · · · · · · · · · · 58
Personal and Family Relationships · · · · · · · · · · · · · · · · 58
Family Relationships · 58
Personal Relationships · 60
Life and Career Reflections · · · · · · · · · · · · · · · · · · 61
Legacy and Impact of Art · 61
Personal Difficulties and Resilience · · · · · · · · · · · · · · · 62
Choosing Between Fame and Authenticity · · · · · · · · · 63
Legacy and Prospects · 64

Chapter 10 · 66
The Last Act and Its Legacy · · · · · · · · · · · · · · · · · · · 66

    Last Years and Death ························66

    Bequests and Contributions ···················· 67

    Shane MacGowan Tribute ·····················69

Conclusion ···72

Closing Remarks and Impact on the Music Industry* ·· 72

    Personal and Creative Legacies ···················74

Acknowledgments ···78

Introduction

Shane MacGowan name has become associated with the dynamic combination of Irish folk and punk rock, and he has made an unforgettable influence on the music business. Shane MacGowan was born on December 25, 1957, in Pembury, Kent, England, to Irish parents, Maurice and Therese MacGowan. His early upbringing was shaped by the rich tapestry of Irish culture that would later form a cornerstone of his musical identity.

Background and Childhood

Shane grew up in Tipperary and then moved to London, where he encountered a fusion of Irish traditions set against the bustling background of the English metropolis. His parents, both of whom were raised in Ireland, were influential in establishing his affinity for the folk songs and narrative that would eventually define his songwriting.

Traditional Irish music provided the soundtrack to Shane's formative years in the MacGowan home, which was a melting pot of influences. The rich oral heritage of storytelling, a staple of Irish culture, grabbed him and became woven into the fabric of his artistic expression. Despite its physical distance from Ireland, the MacGowan home became a haven for Irish customs, establishing the groundwork for Shane's eventual musical study of these topics.

Musical Career Overview

Shane's musical career began in the early 1980s, when he co-founded the band The Pogue Mahone. This was the beginning of a musical adventure that would push boundaries and reinvent genres. The Pogue Mahone, subsequently reduced to The Pogues, emerged as a trailblazing force, blending punk rock's rebellious fury with the timeless charm of Irish folk.

"Red Roses for Me," the band's debut album, released in 1984, exemplified the raw, unfettered attitude that would come to define MacGowan's musical approach. It mixed rowdy versions of classic Irish folk tunes with MacGowan's own compositions. This was the start of a musical journey that would lead The Pogues to international recognition.

Importance and Impact

Shane MacGowan's contributions to music are significant not only for the particular sound he created with The Pogues, but also for his unrivaled com-positional prowess. His songs were a tapestry of gritty reality and heartbreaking narrative, encapsulating the essence of the human experience with a raw honesty that touched audiences all across the world.

The influence of MacGowan's work, both as the leader of The Pogues and as a solo artist, spans genre. The Pogues' distinct fusion of Irish folk and punk rock paved the way for a new wave of musical experimentation, influencing future generations of musicians who wanted to challenge norms and embrace varied cultural influences.

"Fairytale of New York," possibly The Pogues' most famous song, exemplifies MacGowan's ability to capture the complexities of human emotions. This Christmas carol, released in 1987, broke expectations by delivering a harsh story that contrasted dramatically with customary holiday sounds. Its continued popularity solidifies MacGowan's position as a visionary artist who is not hesitant to defy accepted standards.

Beyond the music, Shane MacGowan's life story exemplifies perseverance in the face of adversity. His difficulties with substance misuse and health issues were important chapters in his story, giving sensitivity to his public presence. But it was his vulnerability that drew him to admirers, building a strong bond via the shared human experience of victory and tragedy.

We delve into the roots of Shane MacGowan's rebellious spirit in the following chapters, tracing the trajectory of his musical career, exploring the highs and lows of his personal journey, and ultimately celebrating the enduring legacy of a man who dared to blend the scaly and the sentimental in the symphony of life.

THOMAS K. CLINTON

Chapter 1:

Rebel Roots

Family History

Shane MacGowan's musical career is deeply intertwined within the fabric of his family's rich Irish background. Shane was the first child of Maurice and Therese MacGowan, born on Christmas Day 1957. The MacGowans, originally from County Tipperary in Ireland, brought with them the traditions, legends, and songs that would become the foundation of Shane's rebellious musical identity.

Maurice MacGowan, a fervent defender of Irish cultural history, exemplified the mix of tradition and revolt that would later define Shane's musical style. Maurice instilled in his son a strong respect for the old tales and music that rang through the Irish countryside, having grown up in a region rich in myth and tradition. The MacGowan home in Kent, England, provided a haven for Irish culture to blaze brightly against the backdrop of a new place.

Shane's mother, Therese MacGowan, was equally influential in constructing the family mythology. Shane's blossoming artistic spirit was nurtured by her love of Irish folk music and devotion to preserve the family's cultural tradition. Shane first heard the lovely melodies of traditional Irish ballads and the intriguing anecdotes that accompanied them within the walls of their house.

The family's ties to Ireland remained a constant throughout their life. Shane witnessed the genuineness of Irish life via regular travels to Tipperary, establishing a profound sense of connection to a legacy that transcended physical limits. Like many Irish expats, the MacGowans carried Ireland in their hearts, an unseen country that revealed itself in the cadence of their speech, the warmth of their hospitality, and the resonance of their music.

The MacGowan residence was more than just a physical structure; it was a vessel that carried Shane to Ireland's lush landscapes and mythical regions while navigating the hectic streets of England. Shane's growing identity was forged in the furnace of being Irish in an English context, generating a link to both countries that would resonate strongly in his music.

Early Musical Influences and Inspiration

Shane MacGowan's musical career began with a harmonic tango between classic and contemporary styles. He absorbed the ageless melodies of Irish folk music that rang through the hills of Tipperary. Fiddles, tin whistles, and bodhran became his childhood companions, imprinting a musical lexicon on him that would later find expression in the chaos of punk rock.

Shane's young mind was left with an everlasting mark by the small gatherings in Ireland where musicians and storytellers congregated. The communal aspect of Irish music informed his idea of music's transforming potential, where each note conveyed a narrative and every rhythm connected with shared history. The seeds of insurrection were sowed in these gatherings, as the spirit of Irish music defied time and geographical boundaries.

The 1960s counter-cultural movements introduced Shane MacGowan to a fresh wave of musical revolt as he crossed the terrain of his formative years. Punk rock's disruptive sounds, with their raw energy and anti-establishment spirit, struck a chord with Shane's growing feeling of resistance. This meeting of traditional Irish folk and punk's rebellious spirit established the basis for the alchemical combination that would characterize The Pogues' distinct sound. Shane's adolescence was spent on the streets of London, which became a melting pot of different influences. Shane engaged himself in the rich tapestry of music, fashion, and social turmoil offered by the city's various subcultures. It was in the midst of this kaleidoscope of encounters that his musical personality began to emerge. Shane's creative fire was driven by the conflict of traditionalism and modernity, Irish mythology and punk revolt. His early inspirations, which ranged from melancholy songs of Irish culture to the visceral intensity of punk, provided the canvas with which he would paint The Pogues' aural landscapes.

Shane MacGowan's defiant spirit finds resonance not just in the rebellious chords of punk, but also in the robust heartbeat of Irish folk in the furnace of London's metropolitan surroundings. The various aspects of his musical background fused into a unique vision as he negotiated the maze of self-discovery – a vision that would give birth to The Pogues and revolutionize the possibilities of musical fusion.

In the following chapters, we dig into the transformational years when Shane MacGowan began on the construction of The Pogue Mahone, fuelled by the rebellious soul of his beginnings, laying the stage for a musical revolution that would resound through the annals of rock history.

Chapter 2

Pogue Mahone's Period (1982-1984)

The Pogue Mahone's Formation

In the early 1980s, a group of artists led by Shane MacGowan started on a musical enterprise that would transcend genres and confound expectations, among London's bustling punk and post-punk scenes. The Pogues' origins may be traced back to the 1982 establishment of The Pogue Mahone, which featured Spider Stacy, Jem Finer, James Fearnley, Cait O'Riordan, Andrew Ranken, and Shane himself.

The term "Pogue Mahone" itself mirrored Shane's irreverent and rebellious nature. The moniker, derived from the Irish phrase "póg mo thóin," which means "kiss my arse," marked a break from convention and a dedication to embracing the unashamed blend of Irish folk and punk. The band's name embodied not just their resistance, but also the contagious energy that would become their signature.

Early performances by The Pogue Mahone in London's lively club scene drew attention for their electric stage presence and unique sound. The Pogue Mahone became a musical force to be reckoned with as news spread about their diverse combination of traditional Irish instruments colliding with the raw energy of punk.

The Pogues' Evolution

The transition from The Pogue Mahone to The Pogues was a watershed moment in the band's career. The band's name was changed due to worries about its possible offensiveness, yet this did not dampen its rebellious spirit. Instead, it became a symbol of the band's capacity to overcome obstacles while maintaining their own individuality.

Shane MacGowan was unmistakably fronted, with Spider Stacy on tin whistle, Jem Finer on banjo, James Fearnley on accordion, Cait O'Riordan on bass, and Andrew Ranken on drums. This tight-knit group, driven by a similar desire to push musical limits, lay the framework for The Pogues' rise to stardom.

Shane MacGowan's transition into The Pogues reflected his personal path of self-discovery and artistic development. The transition from "Pogue Mahone" to "The Pogues" signaled not just a name change but also a development of the band's identity. It demonstrated their capacity to adapt and grow while remaining committed to the fundamental aspects that constituted their music.

Musical Influences and Style

The Pogues' musical approach was a strong alchemy of Irish traditional origins and punk's rebellious mentality. The band's style was fundamentally a celebration of contrasts - the clash of old and new, the union of ancient folk melodies with the searing fire of punk rock.

Shane MacGowan's unusual vocal delivery, with its gravelly and expressive texture, became a defining feature of The Pogues' sound. His lyrics, a literary tapestry that blended tales of love, grief, and societal observations, displayed a great awareness of Irish storytelling traditions.

The Pogues used a wide range of traditional Irish instruments in their music. The folk-infused backbone was given by Spider Stacy's tin whistle, Jem Finer's banjo, and James Fearnley's accordion, while the rhythm section, led by Cait O'Riordan's bass and Andrew Ranken's drums, gave a punk rock heartbeat to the mix.

The Pogues' musical inspirations were diverse, drawing inspiration from both Irish traditional traditions and the anarchic spirit of punk. The seamless incorporation of these seemingly incongruous components demonstrated the band's ability to transcend genre boundaries and produce a sound that was both distinct and broadly appealing.

The band's live performances grew famous for their ferocity and passion as they mastered their technique. The Pogues were a force of nature on stage, enthralling listeners with their contagious zeal and the pure delight they gained from their musical combination.

"Red Roses for Me" Debut Album

The Pogues released their debut album, "Red Roses for Me," in 1984, laying the groundwork for their illustrious career. The record, released on Stiff Records, encapsulated the core of The Pogues' musical vision – a riotous celebration of Irish culture infused with punk energy.

The title of the album, taken from Sean O'Casey's play "Juno and the Paycock," alluded to the band's literary interests. The songs on the album were a combination of classic Irish folk tunes and original compositions, with each piece demonstrating Shane MacGowan's growing songwriting talent.

"Red Roses for Me" demonstrated The Pogues' musical range. Tracks like "Transmetropolitan" and "Streams of Whiskey" demonstrated the band's ability to mix classic melodies with a punk mentality, resulting in a sound that was both nostalgic and modern. Shane's lyrics, which were frequently lyrical and rich in imagery, elevated the album above just musical expression to a narrative experience.

The critical response to "Red Roses for Me" was extremely favorable, with many praising The Pogues for their boldness and creativity. The album's popularity provided the framework for the band's following albums and cemented their place as folk-punk fusion trailblazers.

The Pogues' turbulent path through their successes, difficulties, and timeless masterpieces that would carve their name in the annals of musical history is explored in the following chapters.

Chapter 3

Songwriting Prowess of MacGowan

Theme and Songwriting Process

Shane MacGowan's songwriting ability is a shining example of his artistic genius, a talent that transcended musical traditions and spoke directly to the human experience. Dive into the complexity of his songwriting process and you'll find a tapestry woven with strands of tradition, rebellion, and an unfettered examination of life's complexities.

An alchemical mingling of elements was at the heart of MacGowan's songwriting. His creative approach frequently began with absorption in the rich traditions of Irish folk music, gaining inspiration from melodies and stories passed down through generations. Traditional songs provided as a foundation as well as a departure point for him, allowing him to imbue his compositions with a timeless character while still giving them a distinct, modern edge.

According to MacGowan, his songs were a mirror of the human condition, expressing the essence of love, grief, desire, and the harsh truths of life. The distillation of these universal concepts into lyrical tales was both intuitive and methodical.

His words revealed a great observant eye, as well as an emotional depth that struck a deep chord with listeners.

MacGowan's work was replete with references to Irish identity and cultural pride. Songs like "The Sick Bed of Cuchulainn" and "Thousands Are Sailing" demonstrated his ability to combine historical allusions with modern storylines, resulting in songs that were both steeped in history and relevant to the present. The Pogues' ability to cross generational and cultural differences was aided by this combination of past and present, which was a trademark of MacGowan's songwriting.

Immersion in literature, poetry, and life's different experiences was a frequent part of the process. Drawing on the writings of Irish literary giants such as James Joyce and Samuel Beckett, MacGowan's lyrics surpassed the limitations of popular music, achieving a degree of intellectual brilliance that distinguished him from his colleagues.

Classic Songs and Lyrics

Shane MacGowan's lyrics is arguably best illustrated in The Pogues' classic compositions that have become anthems. "Fairytale of New York," published in 1987, remains a landmark effort and tribute to MacGowan's ability to capture the human experience within the constraints of a song.

The opening words, "It was Christmas Eve, babe, in the drunk tank," set the tone for a story that develops with the raw reality and heartbreaking beauty that MacGowan's songs are known for. The song, a duet with Kirsty MacColl, challenges standard Christmas song tropes by providing a sad contemplation on love, dreams, and the passing of time.

"Dirty Old Town," another masterpiece in The Pogues' repertoire, vividly depicts the spirit of city life. MacGowan's performance of Ewan MacColl's song infuses it with emotional intensity, converting it into a visceral homage to the brutal reality of industrial landscapes.

In "A Pair of Brown Eyes," MacGowan constructs a story that combines personal contemplation with larger themes of love and loss. The title of the song is a reference to the ancient Irish folk ballad "A Pair of Brown Eyes," demonstrating MacGowan's fondness for blending traditional components into his own works.

"Rain Street," from The Pogues' album "Peace and Love," demonstrates a distinct side of MacGowan's poetry. The song, a melancholy contemplation on lost love and the passing of time, develops with poetic beauty that stays with the listener.

These legendary songs not only display MacGowan's poetic skill, but also his flexibility as a songwriter. His lyrics have a depth and honesty that transcend genre boundaries, whether capturing the rowdy energy of a bar sing-along or diving into the emotional subtleties of human relationships.

Inter-Pogues Collaborations

While Shane MacGowan's solo work frequently took center stage, his collaborations with The Pogues brought further layers to the band's aural tapestry. The band members' combined inventiveness, each adding their own musical tastes, pushed the collaborative process to a degree of synergy that established The Pogues' sound. Jem Finer, the band's banjo player, and Spider Stacy, noted for his tin whistle, both played important roles in establishing The Pogues' folk aspects.

Their contributions, which frequently blended effortlessly into MacGowan's songs, gave the band's punk-infused sound a traditional Irish authenticity.

The accordion of James Fearnley supplied a melodic backbone, giving the piece with a traditional resonance. The rhythmic basis was laid down by Andrew Ranken's powerful drumming and Cait O'Riordan's bass playing, providing a blank canvas for MacGowan to paint his lyrical storytelling.

The Pogues' collaborations went beyond musical contributions. The band's togetherness generated an environment where creativity blossomed, inspired by shared experiences and a collective enthusiasm for their work. MacGowan's chemistry with his bandmates became a driving force, propelling The Pogues to new heights in the field of folk-punk fusion.

"Sally MacLennane," a vivacious ode to a fictitious Irish heroine, and "If I Should Fall from Grace with God," a title track that captures the band's mix of Irish traditional melodies with punk intensity, are two notable collaboration compositions. These tracks highlight The Pogues' collaborative genius, with each member's contribution coalescing into a seamless whole, raising the music to a level of collective artistry.

The peaks and dips of The Pogues' career, the importance of MacGowan's songwriting on the band's legacy, and the ongoing influence of his lyrical storytelling in the music landscape are all explored in the following chapters.

Chapter 4

Difficulties and Breaks

Personal Struggles of MacGowan

While Shane MacGowan's musical brilliance shone brightly on the stages he frequented, his personal life was marred by a succession of serious difficulties. These troubles, which ranged from substance misuse to the toll of a demanding lifestyle, cast a shade over his artistry's brilliance.

MacGowan's struggles with alcohol and drugs were well-documented, and they became an important part of his story. The hedonistic excesses that frequently accompany the rock and roll lifestyle had a negative impact on his physical and mental health. MacGowan's internal struggle was inspired by the celebration that powered The Pogues' exuberant concerts.

The cost of fame, as well as the responsibilities of frequent touring, worsened these personal difficulties. The tremendous attention that came with being a leader, along with the responsibilities of keeping the band's creative momentum, resulted to a tumultuous personal life.

MacGowan's personal relationships suffered the brunt of his troubles amid the volatility of the rock and roll lifestyle. While his artistic production flourished, The Pogues' interpersonal dynamics and MacGowan's individual relationships were embroiled in a complicated web of emotional issues.

Effect on Band Dynamics and Interruptions

The Pogues' journey was defined by the dramatic interaction between personal challenges and band dynamics. The band's cohesion suffered as a result of MacGowan's struggles with addiction and the toll it had on his dependability. The delicate combination of inventiveness and anarchy that had powered The Pogues' early success became a cause of conflict.

The band took breaks from time to time, frequently due to MacGowan's desire to handle personal issues. These gaps were both a testimonial to the band members' dedication to their frontman and a reflection of MacGowan's turbulent personal life.

Despite these obstacles, The Pogues were able to reassemble and create outstanding music throughout moments of reunion. The band members' perseverance and dedication to the music they made together became a tribute to The Pogues' enduring spirit.

However, the influence on band dynamics was not entirely negative. The challenges also inspired The Pogues' music's honest sincerity. The raw energy, unrestrained emotions, and rejection of society standards were all aspects of MacGowan's and, by extension, the band's personal conflicts.

Medical Concerns and Rehabilitation

Shane MacGowan endured serious health issues that tested his perseverance in addition to his battles with substance misuse. MacGowan was engaged in a horrific accident in December 2002 that resulted in life-changing injuries. He fell from a first-floor window, injuring his skull and fracturing multiple bones.

This episode was a watershed moment in MacGowan's life. The accident's physical toll necessitated substantial medical intervention, and he faced a lengthy period of recuperation. The injury also rendered him unable to move without the assistance of a wheelchair, adding another degree of difficulty to his already difficult trip.

Despite his physical challenges, MacGowan shown amazing tenacity and dedication during his recuperation. His road to recovery became a symbol of the tenacious spirit that defined both the man and his music. However, the rehabilitation process meant a brief absence from the music industry, ushering in a period of contemplation and healing for MacGowan.

In the years after, MacGowan's health has been a source of concern, and he has experienced new issues that have necessitated medical treatment. The toll of a rigorous work, along with the lingering effects of his personal troubles, shaped a story of perseverance in the face of adversity.

The Pogues as a group were also affected by MacGowan's health problems. The band's brief hiatuses were not merely a reaction to MacGowan's personal difficulties, but also a necessary stop for the entire ensemble to recover and support its frontman.

Chapter 5

New York Fairy-tale and Commercial Success

Development of "Fairy-tale of New York"

Certain songs transcend their status as simple compositions to become cultural milestones in the annals of musical history. "Fairytale of New York," written by Shane MacGowan and Jem Finer, is a monument to music's timeless ability to portray the complexity of human experience.

The story of "Fairytale of New York" began in the early 1980s, when MacGowan and Finer set out to write a Christmas song that defied genre traditions. What resulted was a narrative-driven song set against a harsh, genuine depiction of Christmas in New York. The story, as presented via the characters performed by MacGowan and Kirsty MacColl, was far from traditional Christmas fare, adding a raw and real narrative to the holiday music canon.

MacGowan's poetic brilliance took center stage in producing a story that began with sorrow and blossomed into a heartbreaking contemplation on love, grief, and the passing of time. "It was Christmas Eve, babe, in the drunk tank," the opening line set the tone for a narrative that rang true, surpassing the normal feelings connected with Christmas music.

Kirsty MacColl's decision as MacGowan's duet partner brought dimension to the tune. MacColl's voice matched MacGowan's gravelly delivery, resulting in a subtle emotional interaction. Their connection brought the characters to life, transforming the song into a duet that evolved like a stage production.

Musically, "Fairytale of New York" preserved the folk-punk elements that marked The Pogues' style. Traditional Irish instruments like the accordion and tin whistle provided a timeless aspect to the music, while the orchestration emphasized the emotional intricacies of the story.

Publication and Reception

In 1987, The Pogues released "Fairytale of New York" as a single with Kirsty MacColl. Its release date, right before Christmas, positioned it as an unexpected introduction into the seasonal music landscape. The song, on the other hand, surpassed expectations and reached audiences long beyond the holiday season.

"Fairytale of New York" drew considerable notice upon its debut due to its lyrical depth, unique approach to Christmas themes, and dramatic vocal interaction between MacGowan and MacColl. The song's reaction was a mix of surprise and respect for its departure from the syrupy cliches commonly associated with holiday music.

The song's narrative complexity and emotional resonance were praised by critics. The unorthodox approach to Christmas, vivid characterizations, and fusion of Irish traditional customs with punk sensibilities were hailed as innovative. The song's departure from the typical festive formula and acceptance of a darker, more realistic depiction of the Christmas season distinguishes it as a one-of-a-kind achievement.

Despite the praise, the song sparked significant debate owing to the use of the term "faggot" in the lyrics. However, the song's contextual usage within the narrative, as well as its overall creative worth, helped to a larger comprehension of its message. "Fairytale of New York" has been a fixture in arguments about artistic freedom and sensitivity in the context of Christmas music throughout the years.

Commercial and Critical Success

"Fairy-tale of New York" not only won over critics, but also rose to commercial success, becoming a perennial favorite and chart-topping triumph. The financial success of the song paralleled its critical praise, cementing The Pogues' place in the musical scene.

The record charted well in the United Kingdom, reaching number two on the UK Singles Chart upon its first release in 1987. The song's success lasted, and further re-releases saw it reach the coveted Christmas number one slot on the UK Singles Chart in 1988 and 1991.

"Fairy-tale of New York"'s continuing appeal went beyond the United Kingdom, making it a worldwide phenomenon. Its effect echoed across charts in many nations, cementing The Pogues' international reputation.

Aside from chart success, the song's impact spread into popular culture. Its appearance in a plethora of films, television series, and ads proved to its eternal popularity. The song's unique beginning melody and evocative lyrics became instantly identifiable, giving it a position in the cultural fabric that extended beyond its first publication.

"Fairytale of New York" has continuously received positive reviews from critics. It has included on various lists of the greatest Christmas songs, and is frequently noted as a welcome break from the cloying sweetness that defines most of the holiday music canon. The song's ongoing appeal extends beyond the Christmas season, attesting to its universal themes and the timeless brilliance of MacGowan's music.

Chapter 6

Collaborations and the Pope's Era (1994-2005)

The Popes' Formation

During a lull in The Pogues' turbulent voyage in the mid-1990s, Shane MacGowan started on a new musical chapter by founding The Popes. This phase in MacGowan's career marked a dramatic departure, providing a canvas for musical development beyond the folk-punk fusion that distinguished his earlier years with The Pogues.

The Popes, led by MacGowan, formed as a forum for a wide spectrum of influences. Among the artists on the bill were Paul "Mad Dog" McGuinness, Bernie France, and Danny Heatley. They created a group that allowed MacGowan to explore musical territory outside of The Pogues' unique sound.

The Popes' formation was more than just a musical reinvention; it was also a moment of personal development for MacGowan. The band's name was a tribute to the larger musical landscape, incorporating influences that went beyond the Irish folk and punk genres. MacGowan used The Popes to explore the enormous tapestry of musical traditions that had molded his artistic sensibility.

Projects with Johnny Depp and Sinéad O'Connor

During the Popes period, prominent collaborations added layers of intricacy to MacGowan's musical pallet. During this time, one of the most exciting collaborations was with Hollywood actor Johnny Depp, who shared a passion for music and became a vital component of The Popes.

During live performances and studio recordings, Johnny Depp, an outstanding guitarist, collaborated with MacGowan and The Popes. Depp totally immersed himself in the creative process, pushing their partnership beyond the normal limitations of celebrity musical attempts. The combination of MacGowan's raw vocals and Depp's guitar prowess gave a dynamic layer to The Popes' sound, resulting in a distinct blend of rock, folk, and punk elements.

The partnership with Depp went beyond the stage, as the two developed a true friendship fuelled by their common love of music. Their collaboration highlighted Depp's flexibility as a musician and cemented MacGowan's reputation as a magnet for various and unorthodox artistic collaborations.

Another notable collaboration with The Popes was with the legendary Irish vocalist Sinéad O'Connor. The chemistry between MacGowan and O'Connor was especially noticeable in their performance of "Haunted," a song written by O'Connor and included on The Popes' album "The Snake." The hauntingly beautiful duet showed both performers' expressive abilities, transcending genre barriers and creating a musical environment that rang true.

MacGowan's ability to attract musicians from varied backgrounds was highlighted by her work with Depp and O'Connor, resulting in a musical melting pot that defied easy categorization. These collaborations, which arose from a shared artistic vision and a mutual admiration for pushing creative boundaries, strengthened The Popes' record and broadened MacGowan's aural frontiers.

Musical Style and Evolution

The musical progression shown throughout The Popes era demonstrated MacGowan's openness to explore a wide range of styles. While aspects of The Pogues' folk-punk intensity remained in The Popes' sound, the band went into new territory, integrating elements of rock, blues, and even traces of country.

The Popes' debut album, "The Snake," released in 1995, was a shift from The Pogues' folk-driven aesthetics. The album's inspirations were more diverse, with songs like "That Woman's Got Me Drinking" and "A Mexican Funeral in Paris" evoking a raw, rock-infused spirit. The aural experiments in "The Snake" marked MacGowan's pursuit of diverse musical textures while maintaining the unfettered enthusiasm that distinguished his earlier work.

The Popes' artistic trajectory evolved as they released albums such as "The Crock of Gold" (1997) and "Across the Broad Atlantic" (2001). Traditional Irish melodies, such as "Nancy Whiskey" and "Roddy McCorley," were interpreted by the band with a regard for MacGowan's background while infusing these classics with a contemporary edge.

Tracks like "Black Is the Colour" and "The Rising of the Moon" showcased The Popes' ability to draw from a larger folk past, surpassing the confines of Irish folk-rock. The band's dynamic instrumentation, along with MacGowan's unusual vocal delivery, created a musical environment that rang with both familiarity and inventiveness.

While The Popes' record deviated from The Pogues' hallmark sound, MacGowan's lyrics maintained its narrative complexity. Tracks such as "Church of the Holy Spook" and "Lonesome Highway" highlighted his poetic skills, delving into themes of love, sorrow, and philosophical contemplation.

The Popes era not only highlighted a chapter in MacGowan's artistic development, but also demonstrated his tenacity in the face of personal hardships. The band's energetic and unpredictable live performances were a tribute to MacGowan's everlasting love of live music and his ability to captivate fans with his magnetic stage presence.

Chapter 7

Afterlife and Legacy

Pogues Reunions and Final Years

Shane MacGowan's long career ended with a series of reunions with The Pogues, which added fresh chapters to the band's heritage. Despite the difficulties and brief hiatuses, The Pogues were lured back together by the unbreakable bond between MacGowan and his comrades.

The band's first notable reunion occurred in 2001, signifying their return to the stage after a protracted break. The tour, suitably titled "The Pogues: The Ultimate Reunion Tour," brought together the original lineup, including MacGowan, for a series of thrilling concerts. The tour not only renewed The Pogues' live charm, but it also rekindled the spark of their collaborative creativity.

The Pogues revisited their legendary albums during these reunion gigs, offering fans to live renditions of favorites like "If I Should Fall from Grace with God" and, of course, "Fairytale of New

York." The camaraderie between MacGowan and the band remained evident, with their onstage chemistry reminiscent of The Pogues' early years.

The success of the reunion tour led to other engagements, each of which reaffirmed The Pogues' standing as a landmark force in folk-punk. The band's ability to meld traditional Irish melodies with the rebellious spirit of punk grabbed listeners all over the world once again.

MacGowan's participation in these reunions demonstrated not only his tenacity, but also his enduring dedication to the music that had become associated with his name. The Pogues' latter years, punctuated by reunions, provided a new generation of fans with the opportunity to experience the enchantment that marked the band's heyday.

MacGowan remained a captivating presence on stage over the years, defying the passage of time with his ardent performances. The Pogues' final years were a monument to the enduring impact of a band that had established its own space in music history.

Contemporary Music Influence

Shane MacGowan's effect on modern music goes far beyond The Pogues' legacy. His particular combination of Irish folk traditions and punk sensibilities has left a lasting effect on the alternative and folk-rock environment. The influence of MacGowan's composition, vocal style, and genre-defying attitude can be seen in the work of innumerable musicians inspired by his legacy.

One significant facet of MacGowan's effect is the ongoing popularity and cultural relevance of "Fairytale of New York." The song has become a perennial classic and a mainstay of different playlists, far from being limited to the festive season. Its ageless nature, along with MacGowan's powerful narration, has firmly established it as one of the best Christmas songs of all time.

MacGowan's raw, unfiltered feeling has encouraged a new generation of musicians to explore the expressive capabilities of their own voices. His ability to imbue songs with a profound, even visceral sense of emotion has struck a chord with performers from folk to rock to alternative.

The blending of traditional folk elements with punk intensity, which is a characteristic of MacGowan's style, has encouraged bands looking to break free from genre boundaries. The notion that music may be a dynamic, ever-changing dialogue between tradition and revolt remains a motivating factor in the exploration of new sound frontiers.

MacGowan's work with musicians such as Johnny Depp and Sinéad O'Connor further demonstrate his influence on creating unorthodox musical collaborations. His ability to bring musicians from several disciplines together, resulting in a melting pot of creative energy, has established a precedent for joint projects in the ever-changing scene of contemporary music.

MacGowan's lyrical narrative has impacted a generation of artists outside the sphere of music. His ability to create narratives that are both emotional and gritty, lyrical and visceral, has established a precedent for others who want to utilize music as a vehicle for social criticism and storytelling.

with order to understand MacGowan's impact on modern music, it is necessary to acknowledge the esteem with which he is held by his peers. His influence transcends mere style emulation; it is a genuine recognition of the spirit of rebellion, sincerity, and narrative that characterizes his artistic legacy.

The chapters of Shane MacGowan's latter years and legacy continue to emerge as he celebrates his enduring effect on the world of music. His impact may be heard in the work of musicians who, inspired by his pioneering spirit, carry forth the torch of creativity and authenticity in the ever-changing fabric of musical expression.

Chapter 8

Recognition, Awards, and Cultural Impact

Awards and Recognition

Shane MacGowan's exceptional career, highlighted by his distinct contributions to folk-punk and alternative rock, has garnered him a flurry of prizes and distinctions that reflect his music's significant effect on the cultural environment. MacGowan's influence has been recognized via many honors, ranging from critical acclaim for his songwriting to the ongoing success of The Pogues' anthems.

One of MacGowan's most famous honors stems from the ongoing success of "Fairytale of New York." The song, a Christmas favorite that defies tradition, has gained enormous acclaim and has routinely been on lists of the best holiday tunes. The countless accolades and medals showered upon it throughout the years attest to its ongoing appeal.

"Fairytale of New York" has received Platinum accreditation from agencies such as the British Phonographic Industry (BPI) for its ongoing success and significance. The song's capacity to reverberate beyond decades, along with its chart-topping success, elevates it to the pantheon of musical creations.

The Pogues' album "Rum Sodomy & the Lash," released in 1985, was another major milestone for the band. The album, which includes songs like "Dirty Old Town" and "Sally MacLennane," was well praised for its blend of Irish folk traditions with punk vigor. Such acclaim established The Pogues as a major presence in the worlds of alternative and folk-rock music.

Shane MacGowan has been recognized for his songwriting abilities and influence in the music business. His admission into the Songwriters Hall of Fame in 2022 reflects the ongoing power of his lyrical storytelling. This prominent institution's acknowledgment highlights MacGowan's ability to write songs that transcend genres and connect with people on a deep level.

Beyond formal recognition, MacGowan's impact may be seen in the adoration of fellow artists and industry peers. The admiration he receives from the music world is an intangible accolade, recognizing his position as a trailblazer who changed the frontiers of folk and punk music.

Cultural Influence and Impact

Shane MacGowan and The Pogues' cultural impact stretches far beyond the bounds of conventional music prizes. Their impact has spread throughout popular culture, leaving an everlasting stamp on how we perceive and experience music.

This cultural effect is centered on the aforementioned "Fairytale of New York." With its unique Christmas story and emotional storytelling, the song has become a cultural icon. Its annual return on the airways and playlists over the holiday season attests to its ongoing cultural impact. The song's influence has surpassed the boundaries of the music business, becoming a part of the cultural fabric.

The Pogues' blend of Irish traditional music with punk rock had a long-lasting influence on the folk and alternative rock genres. Their ability to integrate traditional instruments, like as accordion and tin whistle, with electric guitars and dynamic rhythms has encouraged future generations of musicians to push genre boundaries.

The Pogues' music's rebellious energy, along with MacGowan's uncompromising and honest poetry, has connected with fans seeking authenticity in an era typified by polished and marketed performances. This honesty has served as a beacon for artists traversing the perilous landscape of artistic expression.

The work of bands and artists that draw inspiration from MacGowan's particular style demonstrates his effect on modern music. Traces of MacGowan's influence may be found in the aural tapestries of many musical environments, whether in the emotional delivery of vocals, the blending of folk elements into alternative rock, or the investigation of unorthodox subjects in songwriting.

The cultural influence of MacGowan's collaborations, notably with Johnny Depp and Sinćad O'Connor during The Popes era, is also significant. These collaborations, born of a common love of music, reflect the collaborative spirit that characterizes the creative process. The desire to experiment with unexpected pairings and bring together performers from many genres demonstrates MacGowan's ongoing impact.

Another aspect of MacGowan's cultural significance is his influence on fashion and style. His particular style, defined by disheveled elegance and a touch of irreverence, has become famous. The blend of traditional Irish costume with punk aesthetics represents the varied character of his music, and this sartorial impact can be noticed in individuals who respect his particular style.

MacGowan's imprint is also seen in the investigation of Irish identity and heritage in music in the larger cultural scene. The Pogues' ability to instill a feeling of Irish pride and heritage in their music while simultaneously questioning prejudices has established a precedent for musicians who want to traverse the intricacies of cultural representation via their work.

As we go deeper into MacGowan's career and the significance of his long legacy, it becomes evident that his cultural influence transcends eras and genres. Instead, it echoes through the fabric of music, motivating musicians to embrace honesty, defy norms, and leave a sound legacy that transcends time and tradition.

Chapter 9

Reflections and Personal Life

Personal and Family Relationships

Shane MacGowan's personal life is characterized by a complicated interplay of victories and hardships that is woven into the fabric of his creative journey. His familial and personal relationships give insights into the man behind the music, illustrating the complexities of a life formed by passion, tenacity, and the quest of artistic expression.

Family Relationships

Shane MacGowan's family history had a huge impact on his identity and worldview. MacGowan was born on Christmas Day in 1957 in Pembury, Kent, England, the son of Irish immigrants. His parents, Maurice and Therese MacGowan, instilled in him a strong attachment to his Irish background, which would later become central to his artistic expression.

Growing up in the United Kingdom, MacGowan was influenced by both Irish culture and the punk movement that was gaining traction in the late 1970s. These formative years paved the way for his distinctive mix of traditional Irish folk with the rebellious spirit of punk rock, a fusion that would define his musical legacy.

However, family dynamics were not without difficulties. The difficulty of integrating his creative aspirations with his family's expectations and worries highlighted MacGowan's journey. The battle between tradition and rebellion reflected the challenges involved in managing the junction of personal and familial identity in his music.

While his family's support was laced with trepidation at times, it became a source of strength for MacGowan. The perseverance instilled in him by his Irish ancestors, together with the freedom granted to him by his family to follow his creative pursuits, laid the groundwork for a life committed to the pursuit of artistic expression.

Personal Relationships

MacGowan's personal connections, both romantic and platonic, have drawn a lot of attention. His relationship with Victoria Mary Clarke, an Irish journalist and writer, became an important element of his personal life. The two had a strong friendship, with Clarke frequently acting as a rock in the face of MacGowan's professional and personal troubles.

The story of MacGowan's life also involves instability, which is frequently entwined with the highs and lows of the music industry. His recognized problems with substance misuse added a degree of complication to his personal connections. The stresses imposed by his demanding profession and the toll of his personal troubles established a backdrop against which his interpersonal dynamics developed.

Despite the difficulties, MacGowan's personal connections were filled with joy, camaraderie, and shared creativity. His partnerships with other musicians, such as Johnny Depp and Sinéad O'Connor, demonstrated the breadth of his abilities to build significant connections outside of traditional relationships.

Shane Oisin MacGowan's birth in 2017 was a poignant chapter in MacGowan's personal life. As he handled the obligations of fatherhood while continuing his artistic aspirations, being a father later in life added additional aspects to his identity. The cyclical aspect of life provided a dimension of reflection to MacGowan's own tale, with a new generation developing as he completed his trip.

Life and Career Reflections

Shane MacGowan's comments on his life and work, as one of the most prominent personalities in alternative and folk-rock music, provide an insight into the mind of an artist whose influence stretches well beyond the bounds of his songs.

Legacy and Impact of Art

MacGowan's thoughts on his creative legacy indicate a deep knowledge of the societal significance of his music. The ageless resonance of "Fairytale of New York" and the continued popularity of The Pogues' anthems are indicators of a legacy that transcends time.

MacGowan has frequently highlighted the emotional and raw aspect of his songs in interviews. His lyrics, which feature a unique combination of critical social commentary, sensitive love ballads, and images of life's grittier realities, highlight his devotion to creative honesty.

The Pogues' style was defined by a musical cocktail of Irish traditional music and punk rock, a tribute to MacGowan's ability to manage the nuances of cultural identification. His views on the junction of Irish history and punk ethos indicate a concerted attempt to question established conceptions and carve out a space in music for alternative narratives.

Personal Difficulties and Resilience

MacGowan's personal battles with drug misuse and health concerns give insight into the difficulties he endured throughout his life. The toll of a difficult profession, combined with the pressures of celebrity, resulted in moments of volatility that were frequently played out in public.

His perseverance in the face of adversity becomes a recurring motif in his recollections. MacGowan's tenacious spirit is shown in his capacity to confront personal demons, endure rehabilitation, and emerge with a fresh sense of purpose. The recovery procedure following his 2002 accident, which left him wheelchair-bound, constituted a watershed moment in his life, stressing the resilience necessary to overcome hardship.

Choosing Between Fame and Authenticity

In MacGowan's comments, the complications of negotiating celebrity and retaining authenticity emerge as important topics. The scrutiny that comes with popularity, along with the music industry's expectations, caused a conflict between the commercial needs of the mainstream and the desire to stay faithful to his creative vision.

MacGowan's disdain for industry rules is reflected in his outspoken approach to music-making. The reluctance to dilute the raw intensity of his performances or compromise the purity of his songs indicates a dedication to authenticity that has resonated with fans looking for true artistic expression.

MacGowan has frequently voiced disgust for the trappings of celebrity culture in interviews. His unwillingness to adhere to the expectations of the media and the business reflects a desire to exist on his own terms, free of the superficialities that are typically connected with celebrity.

Legacy and Prospects

As MacGowan considers his legacy, he feels both satisfaction and reflection. The influence of his music, the acknowledgment of his songwriting abilities, and the continuing affection for The Pogues' songs are all sources of pride for him. However, the contemplative tenor of his interviews implies that he is always exploring the difficulties that constitute a life committed to artistic expression.

Looking ahead, MacGowan's comments on the future of music suggest optimism tempered by a realistic awareness of the industry's ever-changing character. The cyclical nature of creation, the development of new voices, and the natural reinvention inherent in the artistic process are themes that highlight a feeling of continuity that extends beyond his own contributions.

The complexity of Shane MacGowan's journey become clearer as we read through the chapters of his personal life and observations. It is a story distinguished by passion, resilience, and an unwavering devotion to authenticity—an examination of identity, creativity, and the never-ending search for meaning via the medium of music.

Chapter 10

The Last Act and Its Legacy

Last Years and Death

The final act of Shane MacGowan's illustrious life was distinguished by a tapestry of tenacity, creative legacy, and a tremendous effect on the music industry. MacGowan's latter years were distinguished by both the long problems he encountered and the irrepressible energy that defined his image.

For many years, the musician's health had been a source of concern, with different episodes showing the toll of a life lived on the edge. The 2015 injury that limited MacGowan to a wheelchair became a symbol of his physical problems. He was hospitalized in December 2022 with viral encephalitis, aggravating his health problems. Despite these failures, MacGowan's spirit remained unbroken, and he carried on with the same irreverence that distinguished his music.

Shane MacGowan's death on a December morning signaled the end of an era—a time when the world said goodbye to a musical giant whose impact crossed borders. MacGowan's demise, surrounded by his family, was a devastating reminder of the fragility of life and the enduring power of artistic legacy.

Bequests and Contributions

Shane MacGowan's history exemplifies the transformational power of music, and it goes beyond chart-topping records and industry honors. His contributions to the musical scene have left an everlasting impact on the hearts of listeners and the growth of genres, created by a unique combination of Irish folk, punk rock, and raw poetry.

The Pogues' catalog, a collection of recordings that resisted easy categorization, lies at the heart of MacGowan's legacy. From the riotous fervor of "Red Roses for Me" to the anthemic resonance of "If I Should Fall from Grace with God" and the timeless charm of "Fairytale of New York," each album represented a chapter in a musical journey that continues to be unsurpassed in its range and emotional depth.

The Pogues had an incalculable influence on folk-punk, with their ability to flawlessly merge traditional Irish instruments with punk sensibilities affecting generations of performers. Their concerts' raw, unfiltered energy set a benchmark for authenticity in a music scene dominated by polished productions.

MacGowan's solo work and collaborations with The Popes contributed to his legacy outside of The Pogues. The desire to experiment with new genres, interact with musicians from various backgrounds, and evolve as a musician demonstrated a dedication to pushing creative limits. Songs like "That Woman's Got Me Drinking" and "Haunted" with Sinéad O'Connor demonstrate the breadth of his post-Pogues artistic journey.

"Fairytale of New York" is MacGowan's crowning achievement, a timeless song that has become synonymous with the Christmas season. Its cultural significance, which spans decades and cultural barriers, illustrates the lasting power of music-based storytelling. The song's ability to portray the complexity of love, sorrow, and hope has propelled it to eternal relevance.

Songs like "A Pair of Brown Eyes," "Dirty Old Town," and "The Broad Majestic Shannon" showcase MacGowan's songwriting skill. These songs, distinguished by vivid storytelling and an acute awareness of human emotions, demonstrate the breadth and flexibility of his poetry.

Shane MacGowan Tribute

Remembering Shane MacGowan is a chance to honor a life committed to artistic expression, disobedience of standards, and an unwavering devotion to authenticity. Fans, other artists, and industry peers paid tribute, all emphasizing that MacGowan's significance extends beyond the bounds of the music industry.

His contribution to the Irish cultural environment is enormous, as he reshaped the story of Irish identity via song. The Pogues' ability to instill Irish pride in their music while defying preconceptions and adopting a punk attitude has impacted future generations of musicians exploring the intersections between tradition and rebellion.

The music world lamented the departure of a pioneer who crossed the gap between folk and punk, honesty and commercial success, with a slurred yet forceful voice. As condolences and praises poured in on social media, it became clear that MacGowan's influence was not limited to a specific era or demographic.

The Popes, Johnny Depp, Sinéad O'Connor, and many others who have worked with MacGowan expressed heartfelt remarks on his influence on their lives and the music business. These testimonies portrayed a musician who inspired not only via his music but also by his genuineness, perseverance, and willingness to embrace the unexpected.

Fans returned to The Pogues' history, digging into choruses that had become anthems of rebellion, love, and Christmas, and there was a communal acknowledgement that MacGowan's voice, both as a poet and singer, had left an everlasting impression on the hearts of millions.

Shane MacGowan's long legacy is found not just in the chords of his guitar or the lyrics of his songs, but also in the cultural influence he had on people's perceptions of what music might be. His unwillingness to conform, appreciation of flaws, and ability to find beauty in the worst aspects of life struck a chord with a worldwide audience.

The curtain may have collapsed in the final act of Shane MacGowan's life, but the echoes of his defiant spirit live on. His legacy lives on in the generations of musicians who find inspiration in his unashamed attitude to creating, in the listeners who play The Pogues' recordings with nostalgia, and in the larger landscape of music that he helped form.

We remember Shane MacGowan as the embodiment of a philosophy—one that encourages honesty, celebrates variety, and believes in the transformational potential of music as a vehicle for narrative and connection. Shane MacGowan is a timeless presence in the chapters of his life and legacy, whose impact stretches well beyond the notes and chords that make his songs.

Conclusion

Closing Remarks and Impact on the Music Industry*

Shane MacGowan emerges as a dynamic thread in the broad fabric of music history, sewn with the spirit of revolt, the resonance of raw poetry, and the fusion of genres that defied convention. When we consider MacGowan's effect on the music business, it becomes clear that his voyage was more than simply a musical expedition; it was a transforming force that left an indelible stamp on the very core of creative expression.

MacGowan's impact on the music business is multidimensional, involving aural invention, cultural reinterpretation, and an unwavering dedication to authenticity. The revolutionary synthesis of Irish traditional music with punk rock by The Pogues not only reinvigorated folk-punk but also lay the framework for a larger investigation of genre boundaries. Their ability to fluidly blend classical instruments with the rebellious spirit of punk created a precedent for musicians looking to disrupt established standards.

The effect of The Pogues' catalog, highlighted by songs like "Fairytale of New York," goes beyond traditional chart success criteria. It lives on in the hearts of followers who found consolation, inspiration, and a feeling of defiance in MacGowan's uncensored storytelling. The music of The Pogues became a cultural icon, engaging with listeners across generations and transcending time and trends.

MacGowan's uncompromising approach to his art, defined by a slurred yet forceful vocal delivery and lyrics that addressed the brutal truths of existence, was a challenge to the polished aesthetics that pervade the music business. His reluctance to comply to accepted conventions, as well as his embracing of flaws, marked a divergence from the manufactured perfection frequently associated with mainstream success.

The significance of MacGowan's collaborations, whether with The Pogues, The Popes, or performers like as Johnny Depp and Sinéad O'Connor, adds to the story of his impact. These collaborations demonstrated not just his flexibility as a musician, but also his ability to develop creative alliances that crossed traditional borders. The desire to explore other musical environments and cooperate with musicians from various genres demonstrated a dedication to pushing artistic limits.

MacGowan's influence on the music business extends beyond his musical talents to his status as a cultural figure. His particular style, defined by unkempt elegance and a touch of irreverence, became renowned in its own right. The blend of traditional Irish garb with punk aesthetics highlighted not just a stylistic decision, but also a visual depiction of his music's varied character.

Personal and Creative Legacies

Shane MacGowan's legacy extends beyond the platforms he graced and the recordings he produced. It lives on in the hearts of people who found inspiration in his rejection of norms, consolation in his words, and resonance in his music. As we delve into his personal and creative legacy, we peel back the layers of a life committed to the quest of honesty and the transformational power of music storytelling.

His unrelenting devotion to sincerity lies at the heart of MacGowan's legacy. His reluctance to compromise the raw intensity of his performances, the uncensored quality of his lyrics, and The Pogues' unique sound represent an artist who valued creative integrity over financial considerations. This dedication has left an indelible mark on the spirit of creative expression, pushing a new generation of artists to embrace flaws and appreciate the uniqueness of their voices.

MacGowan's reputation is inextricably linked to the development of folk-punk, a genre he helped define and enhance. The Pogues' ability to inject punk energy into traditional Irish songs reinvigorated folk music, offering up new options for experimentation and genre fusion. His songwriting talent, characterized by profound storylines and a deep awareness of the human experience, has established a precedent for those who regard music as a way of storytelling.

The long-lasting impact of "Fairytale of New York" demonstrates MacGowan's ability to convey the intricacies of human emotions. Far from being a Christmas hymn, the song has evolved into an eternal depiction of love, sorrow, and the passing of time. Its cultural influence extends beyond music, penetrating popular culture and becoming a perennial favorite in a variety of contexts.

As a songwriter, MacGowan's talents are distinguished by a distinct combination of biting social satire, soft love ballads, and glimpses of life's harsher truths. Tracks like "A Pair of Brown Eyes," "Dirty Old Town," and "The Broad Majestic Shannon" demonstrate his storytelling's depth and flexibility. His ability to create storylines that are universal in nature while being steeped in the distinctiveness of Irish culture is a defining feature of his musical heritage.

Shane MacGowan's personal and creative impact is also evident in the connections he fostered. His collaborations with other artists, both within and outside of The Pogues, demonstrate his capacity to connect and create beyond the boundaries of individual talent. The connection with musicians, the friendship with collaborators like as Johnny Depp, and the shared creative energy with Sinéad O'Connor all point to a legacy that goes beyond solo performances.

The difficulties and personal problems weaved within MacGowan's story add to the richness of his legacy. His fortitude in the face of health challenges, drug misuse troubles, and the demands of fame reflect a spirit that goes beyond artistic accomplishments. The recovery process that followed his 2002 injury, as well as his ability to handle the complexity of human relationships, add dimensions to a legacy that includes both victories and hardships.

There is an invitation in the chapters of Shane MacGowan's personal and creative legacy to reflect not just on the notes and chords that comprise his music, but also on the ethos he represented. It is a heritage that encourages honesty, welcomes flaws, and appreciates music's transformational potential as a vehicle for human expression.

Shane MacGowan's legacy remains an ever-present melody as we negotiate the last chords of our exploration—a reminder that an artist's effect goes well beyond the temporal bounds of their existence. It may be found in the rebellious attitude of people who continue to defy norms, in the sincerity of musicians who find refuge in faults, and in the eternal stories shared via music.

The echoes of Shane MacGowan's legacy remain in the final refrain of this tale, an eternal monument to music's persistent capacity to transcend, transform, and leave an indelible stamp on the ever-evolving canvas of human experience.

Acknowledgments

The completion of this in-depth investigation of Shane MacGowan's life, work, and legacy is a credit to the combined efforts and support of those who contributed in various roles. We are grateful to all whose thoughts, support, and expertise have enhanced our journey.

To begin, we would like to express our heartfelt gratitude to Shane MacGowan's family and close acquaintances, who gave insights and recollections that brought vital context to his life during a difficult time. The sincerity and openness with which MacGowan shared personal parts of his journey allowed for a more nuanced and realistic portrayal.

We'd like to thank the artists and collaborators who graciously expressed their thoughts on working with Shane MacGowan. Their observations gave rare insights into the creative process, The Pogues' dynamics, and the larger influence of MacGowan's partnerships on the music business.

Special gratitude to Shane MacGowan and The Pogues fans who, through their passion and commitment, have maintained and embraced this legendary artist's legacy. Your excitement and dedication to music provided a vivid backdrop for our research.

We thank the journalists, biographers, and historians who have exhaustively recorded Shane MacGowan's life. Your research and documentation have established the framework for this. Your contributions laid the groundwork for this in-depth analysis.

We also want to thank the larger music community, including fellow artists, reviewers, and industry professionals, for helping to define the cultural context in which Shane MacGowan's legacy flourishes.

Printed in Great Britain
by Amazon